Breaking Through
Six More Newnham Lives

Breaking Through
Six More Newnham Lives

EDITED BY

BIDDY PASSMORE

Published by
Newnham College
Cambridge CB3 9DF
www.newn.cam.ac.uk

A CIP catalogue record for this book is available from the
British Library

ISBN 978-0-9930715-1-5

Copy-editing and design Perilla Kinchin, White Cockade Publishing
Printed and bound by TJ International Ltd, Padstow

Front cover: *Millicent Fawcett leads the rally in Hyde Park after the Great
Suffrage Pilgrimage of 1913 (Courtesy of LSE)*

Back cover: *Detail of the gates beneath the Pfeiffer Arch, the original
entrance to the College, erected in memory of the first Principal, Anne
Jemima Clough (1820–92)*

p.2 and p.13: *Students in Newnham College gardens, 1933*

CONTENTS

THE CONTRIBUTORS

JANET BURROWAY (b.1936, NC 1958) is an American author whose published works include novels, memoirs, short stories, poems, plays, children's books and two books about the craft of writing. Her 1969 novel *The Buzzards* was shortlisted for the Pulitzer Prize. *Writing Fiction: A Guide to Narrative Craft* (1982), soon due out in its 10th edition, is the most widely used creative writing text in America. Janet was educated at the University of Arizona and at Barnard College before studying English at Newnham (1958–60) on a Marshall scholarship. She taught at the University of Sussex (1965–70), then Florida State University (1972–2002). She and her husband Peter Ruppert live in Lake Geneva, Wisconsin, and Chicago. She is at work on a ninth novel, *Indian Dancer*.

ISABELLE GREY (b.1954, NC 1973) is a screenwriter, novelist, non-fiction author and former journalist. She read Philosophy and English at Newnham and then became a freelance journalist and author. As Isabelle Anscombe, she has published five books on decorative arts, including *A Woman's Touch: Women in Design from 1860 to the Present Day* (1984) and *Arts & Crafts Style* (1991), before turning to television drama and crime fiction. Her most recent novel, *Wrong Way Home* (2018), is published by Quercus.

SUSIE HARRIES (b.1951, NC 1970) is a writer, lecturer and editor specialising in 20th-century culture and history. She studied Classics and Classical Philosophy at Newnham and St Anne's, Oxford. While working at the RSA she produced the report *Drugs – Facing Facts* (2007). Susie has co-authored seven books with her husband, Meirion Harries, on subjects ranging from opera to war artists. Her most recent book, the biography of Sir Nikolaus Pevsner (2011), won the Wolfson Prize for History 2012 and was widely praised. She is now working on a book about the Great and the Good in post-war Britain.

UNA MCCORMACK (b.1972, NC 1990) is a science fiction author, specialising in tie-in novels based on popular TV series like *Star Trek* and *Doctor Who*; one of her novels has been a *New York Times* bestseller. She is a lecturer in creative writing at Anglia Ruskin University and co-directs its Centre for Science Fiction and Fantasy. After studying History and SPS at Cambridge, she took an MSc in Psychology at Reading and a PhD in Sociology at the University of Surrey. She taught for many years at Judge Business School. She has written a dozen novels and many sci-fi short stories and audio dramas. She lives in Cambridge with her partner and daughter.

JILL NICHOLLS (b.1951, NC 1971) is an award-winning documentary film-maker. She has profiled many leading writers – including Toni Morrison, Judith Kerr, Doris Lessing, Orhan Pamuk and Diana Athill – for the BBC series *Imagine*. She has also made many history films (*Wallis Simpson*, *The Ottoman Harem*, *The Art That Hitler Hated*). Her most lauded work poetically inter-weaves past and present (*Salman Rushdie: The Fatwa Years* and *Vivian Maier: Who Took Nanny's Pictures?*). After gaining a First in English at Newnham, she joined the feminist magazine *Spare Rib* and has always pursued stories about women's lives.

ROSALIND RIDLEY (b.1949, NC 1968) is a scientist, writer and artist. After studying Natural Sciences at Cambridge, she took her PhD in neurophysiology at the Institute of Psychiatry in London. In 1977 she joined the Medical Research Council's scientific staff, moving in 1994 to the Department of Psychology at Cambridge, where she stayed until 2005 as Head of the MRC's Comparative Cognition Research Team. Much of her research has been aimed at treatments for Alzheimer's, Parkinson's and Huntington's diseases. She was a Fellow of Newnham College 1995–2010 and Vice-Principal 2000–5. With her husband, Dr Harry Baker, she wrote *Fatal Protein: The Story of CJD, BSE and other Prion Diseases* (1998). In 2016, she published *Peter Pan and the Mind of J.M. Barrie, An Exploration of Cognition and Consciousness*. Ros has a strong interest in visual perception and her current activities include painting.

EDITOR'S PREFACE

Editing a book of this kind is like childbirth. You forget what it was like last time and merrily volunteer to do it again.

Not until I was some way down the road with *Breaking Through* did I remember how challenging it had been to produce *Breaking Bounds*, pleased as I was with that baby. There's the struggle to find good writers with the time and inclination to research and write a substantial piece about a woman probably unknown to them, however much they love Newnham and however intrigued they are by the idea. There's the heart-breaking moment when a writer who thought she could do it is felled by a pile-up of other deadlines. Even months later, when all is safely commissioned, gathered in and edited, there is illustration hell. An atmospheric photograph is deemed too fuzzy, even for a small page; an arty portrait is not available for love, only for serious money, and the person who could give you permission to use it has disappeared down a rabbit-hole ...

And yet, as with *Breaking Bounds*, the whole project has been made possible, even enjoyable, through the help and support of Newnham alumnae. It would not have got underway at all without encouragement from Penny Hubbard, Newnham's Development Director and the Registrar of the Roll, and help and advice from Jean Gooder, former Director of Studies in English and, one might say, keeper of the EngLit Roll. Anne Thomson, College Archivist, has been a stalwart, spending many hours looking up Roll Letter entries on biographical subjects and digging out wonderful pictures and scanning and sending them with great efficiency. In the Development Office, publishing expert Rebecca Quigg has been calm and helpful.

Special thanks go once again to my editorial advisers and old friends from Newnham days: Susie Harries – who this time also contributed a word-perfect essay herself, despite lecturing all over England, starting a new book and looking after a new grandson – and Perilla Kinchin of White Cockade Publishing, who again nobly took on the design and layout of the book in the midst of many other projects. Many thanks also to my son Luke Ridley for technical assistance, especially with pictures.

But my greatest debt must be to the writers, who agreed with enthusiasm to write a 2,000-word essay for no fee about an unfamiliar subject, kept to their deadlines – and mostly bore it with good humour when I then committed the editorial sin of asking them to write more. They have brought to life six fascinating women, all highly individual and yet, from Millicent Fawcett onwards, all demonstrating the brains, energy, staying-power and wit of the ideal Newnhamite.

Biddy Passmore (NC 1970)

PICTURE CREDITS

Unless otherwise stated, all photographs come from the archives of Newnham College Cambridge and are reproduced with the kind permission of the Principal and Fellows.

Every effort has been made to trace owners and seek permission for the use of other images. We are grateful to the following:

Millicent Garrett Fawcett p.14 Portrait of Millicent Fawcett, 1892 Newnham College Archive; p.18 Courtesy of National Portrait Gallery (NPG); image on cover flap of Millicent at 18, p.20, p.23, p.25 all Courtesy of LSE Library

Susan Lawrence p.28 Portrait extracted from Newnham College group 1898; p.31 Courtesy of LSE library; p.34 Spartacus-Educational.com; p.37, p.38, p.40 all Courtesy of NPG

Marjory Stephenson p.42 Portrait cropped from picture of Marjory with two friends, 1930s Courtesy of Department of Biochemistry, Cambridge; p.46 Miss Stephenson in Salonika © Imperial War Museum; p.48 Courtesy of Department of Biochemistry, Cambridge

Francesca Wilson p.56 Portrait as a young woman © Religious Society of Friends (Quakers) in Britain; p.62 http://mikein-mono.blogspot.com/2015/02/nikolai-bakhtin-nicholas-bachtin.html; p.65 from PhD thesis by Siân Roberts, University of Birmingham: copyright holder could not be traced

Alix Strachey p.68 Portrait from Newnham Cricket XI, see p.72; p.74, p.77, p.79 all Courtesy of NPG

Jacquetta Hawkes p.82 Portrait by Ramsey & Muspratt, Cambridge, p.85, p.87, p.88, p.90 all Courtesy of Special Collections, University of Bradford; p.92 Photograph by Howard Coster, Courtesy of NPG

Introduction

DAME CAROL BLACK

Principal of Newnham College

I am delighted to welcome this second book of Newnham on Newnham: six more biographical essays about fascinating Newnham women of the past by gifted Newnham writers of today.

Breaking Through comes out in a year rich in important anniversaries for British women – and one with particular meaning for Newnhamites. This is the 100th anniversary of The Roll, a 'Register of Old Students' set up in 1918, nearly half a century after the foundation of the College but shortly after it had become a self-governing community with its own statutes and Charter. The Roll is a precious record of the women who have attended or been closely involved with the College, reaching back to its earliest days in the 1870s. It is also, of course, an active alumnae association, keeping Newnhamites in touch with each other, so that the mutually supportive relationships that are the hallmark of the College can continue throughout life.

All the women who feature in these essays 'broke through' in some way: a biochemist who was one of the first two women elected FRS, one of the first women Labour MPs, a pioneering humanitarian, one of the earliest psychoanalysts in Britain … All deserve to be better known. But in this year, as we celebrate the 100th anniversary of the Act that at last gave British women the vote, it seems right to give pride of place in the book – as in Parliament Square – to Dame Millicent Fawcett. This persistent and pragmatic leader of the suffragists did more than anyone else to secure votes for women and, as every Newnhamite knows, she was a co-founder of the College. For her, the enfranchisement of women always involved both the right to vote and access to higher education.

The contributors to this book are a varied sample of Newnham's wealth of good writers. They include authors of biography and fiction – including sci-fi and thrillers – a journalist turned documentary film-maker, a research scientist turned writer and artist, and the queen of creative writing in America. We are very grateful indeed for their time and support for this project. Once again, proceeds from sales of the book will go towards College bursary funds, to help support students across the entire range of subjects studied here.

I hope you enjoy reading it.

Millicent Garrett Fawcett
(1847–1929)

ISABELLE GREY

To celebrate the centenary of the 1918 Representation of the People Act, which gave the first cohort of British women the right to vote, Millicent Garrett Fawcett, leader of the law-abiding suffragists and a co-founder of Newnham College, has become the first woman to be commemorated with a statue in Parliament Square.

Her statue joins those of ten men, including Winston Churchill and Nelson Mandela – the perfect tribute to a woman who lived out her unswerving belief that women had the right to take their place alongside even the most able men in whatever field they chose to enter.

Millicent Fawcett was of small height and was said to appear young throughout her life. Modest, confident and energetic, she enjoyed both needlework and mountaineering, and remained an adventurous traveller well into old age. Although seen as reserved and undemonstrative as she grew older, especially in contrast to the charismatic suffragette leader Emmeline Pankhurst, her eloquence, humour and persistence meant that she emerged as a natural leader in almost any activity in which she chose to be involved.

The most important influence on her life and achievements may well have been the remarkable family into which she was born. Her belief that women's rights and education went hand in hand, and that women would ultimately win the vote by proving themselves responsible and professional enough to be trusted with it, was rooted in the experiences – and amply demonstrated by the pioneering achievements – of her own sisterhood.

She grew up in Aldeburgh, Suffolk, the seventh of ten surviving children of Newson Garrett, a successful, if volatile, entrepreneur, an active and radical Liberal, a self-made man and believer in Self-Help, and his evangelical, capable, and affectionate wife Louisa. The power-house of the family, however, was the second of Millicent's four older sisters, Elizabeth.

Like all the Garrett girls, Elizabeth – ten years older than Millicent – was taught by a governess at home before spending two years from the age of fourteen to sixteen at a school in Blackheath run by Miss Louisa Browning, an aunt of the poet. On a visit to a school friend Elizabeth met Emily Davies, later co-founder and Mistress of Girton, who introduced her to others of the influential 'Langham Place' group associated with both the Society for Promoting the Employment of Women and *The English Woman's Journal*.

In 1859, despite having been taught no science and very little mathematics, Elizabeth was inspired by a meeting with Dr Elizabeth Blackwell (the first woman to receive a medical degree in the United States) to set about obtaining a medical education herself. Her father initially opposed her plans – it was widely considered 'unnatural' for a woman to study anatomy, especially of the male body – and her mother was horrified. However, when medical schools and universities consistently refused his daughter, Newson Garrett – always wilful and quarrelsome – threatened to sue the Society of Apothecaries when they, too, attempted to bar her from their examinations.

In 1865 Elizabeth gained a licence to practise medicine from the Society, making her the first woman qualified in Britain entitled to have her name entered on the medical register. The Society promptly changed its rules so no other woman could follow her.

While she studied in London, Newson had supported Elizabeth financially, as he would her sisters. She also enjoyed the support of her older married sister Louisa. In turn, Elizabeth, now practising as a doctor in Upper Berkeley Street, did her best to encourage independence among other female relatives, first persuading her father to let her sister Alice become a clerk in his business and then trying to find a teaching post for a cousin, Rhoda Garrett. In 1865 Alice married and left for India, leaving their twenty-year-old sister Agnes to be their mother's companion in Aldeburgh. Elizabeth rescued Agnes by offering to pay her £9 a month to be her housekeeper in Upper Berkeley Street. For Elizabeth, still an unmarried young woman, to possess the financial and social independence required to make good such an invitation must have been empowering.

It was at this time that the seventeen-year-old Millicent also came to London to live with Louisa. Both Louisa and Elizabeth were already active in the women's suffrage movement, and Millicent attended meetings at which she heard John Stuart Mill speak on the subject, helped Elizabeth to host a meeting of governesses in support of Emily Davies' campaign to open university exams to women, and, at a party given by radical suffragists, met Henry Fawcett, Cambridge professor of political economy, Liberal MP for Brighton and an active supporter of both electoral reform and women's rights. He and the nineteen-year-old Millicent were married in April 1867.

Ford Maddox Ford, Henry and Millicent Fawcett, 1872 (NPG).

Eight years earlier Henry Fawcett's budding career at the bar had been cut short when he was blinded in a shooting accident. Although his refusal to be limited by his disability in either work or pleasure – he continued to skate and to ride – was remarkable, it also enabled his young wife to support him professionally in public and to educate herself politically. As Elizabeth wrote to a friend, Millicent 'is heartily in love with him so that she will not feel the service a burden'. It was by all accounts a happy marriage.

Henry encouraged Millicent to develop her own speaking and writing career. She wrote and published (as Millicent Garrett Fawcett) throughout her life – social and political essays, biography, fiction and memoir – and her first book, *Political Economy for Beginners*, was a bestseller.

Despite suffering 'cold spasms' beforehand, she gave her first public speech in favour of women's suffrage in 1869. The twenty-two-year-old Mrs Henry Fawcett argued in front of an audience that included John Stuart Mill that women should 'no longer forgo their claims to equality for toys and sugar-plums'. The following year the *Brighton Herald* reported on one of her speeches: 'She's a lady of small stature and a fragile but very pleasing appearance, perfectly collected in her manner and with a clear, distinct, emphatic delivery not at times without a sense of humour.' It was supposedly the sweetness of her voice that had first attracted her future husband.

The star speaker on suffrage in the family, however, with whom Millicent often shared a platform, was her slightly older cousin Rhoda. Much loved by those close to her, Rhoda had more or less to fend for herself after her father remarried following her mother's death. By 1867 she had determined to train as an architect, and was joined in her ambition by Millicent's sister, Agnes.

As Elizabeth had learnt while seeking medical training, Rhoda and Agnes now discovered how difficult it was to find anyone prepared to take women on as clerks. In 1871, however, they became apprenticed to the London architect J.M. Brydon. No doubt their experiences in writing and delivering speeches, organising committees, fund-raising and the other

Rhoda Garrett addresses a women's rights meeting at the Hanover Square
Rooms in 1872. The new Mrs Fawcett listens on the left.

work demanded by the suffrage campaign all helped to prepare
them for the demands of professional life – and vice versa.

While Agnes, Rhoda and Elizabeth were in London
making inroads into hitherto exclusively male professions,
Millicent divided her time between homes in South
London and Cambridge, running both with efficiency and
economy. In her Cambridge drawing room in 1869, as she
'sat on a little stool by the fireside, next to her husband, in
order to give an informal air to the proceedings', they dis-
cussed Henry Sidgwick's scheme to establish a programme
of 'Lectures for Ladies' in Cambridge. She admitted years
later that, 'if we had said we wished to establish a College
for women at Cambridge we might as well have said that
we wished to establish a College for women in Saturn. It
was an absolute necessity to proceed with great caution.'

The success of the lectures, launched the following
year with the support of Sidgwick and Jemima Anne
Clough, allowed them to take the next step and arrange
residential accommodation so that women could at least

meet the conditions required to take University exams. This led to the foundation of Newnham Hall (built by Basil Champneys, an architect who shared offices with J.M. Brydon), which grew to become Newnham College. Millicent helped to raise money, to organise lectures and to attract serious students, not those who would attend 'just for amusement'. She served on the college council for twenty-eight years.

By the time she had turned thirty in 1877, both she and Elizabeth (now Elizabeth Garrett Anderson) had children; Elizabeth had established the New Hospital for Women, joined the teaching staff of the London School of Medicine for Women, and performed surgery; Agnes and Rhoda had opened their own business as 'House Decorators' in Gower Street, published a successful book, *Suggestions for House Decoration* (1876), and were preparing to exhibit at the Universal Exhibition in Paris; Millicent had co-founded Newnham, was active in Liberal politics and had published a novel. The sisters' close familial support, and the opportunity to share practical and emotional experience, must have enhanced their confidence, strength and daring, and made each of them more determined.

Louisa had died of appendicitis in 1867. In 1882 Rhoda died of typhoid, and when, two years later, Henry Fawcett died, the devastated Millicent and her teenage daughter Philippa went to live with Agnes in Gower Street. Agnes also continued to take responsibility for Rhoda's orphaned step-siblings, and the extended family spent school holidays together at Agnes's Sussex cottage. Only after a long period of mourning did Millicent return to public life.

Not content with their own achievements, and their continuing commitment to women's rights, the sisters also did all they could to open doors for other women, offering apprenticeships and devising practical solutions. In 1888 they were behind a scheme to provide lodgings in London for 'unprotected' single professional women. Agnes was the co-founder and director of the Ladies' Residential Chambers Company and Elizabeth and Millicent were shareholders. The architect was J.M. Brydon and the building, in Chenies Street, proved convenient for the Newnham classicist Jane Harrison, who became a tenant when studying at the British Museum.

Millicent and her sisters inevitably influenced the next generation of Garretts. In 1890 Millicent's daughter Philippa Fawcett, the 'apple of her eye and the joy of her heart', a Newnham undergraduate who had inherited her father's mathematical ability, was placed 'above the Senior Wrangler' in the Mathematical Tripos. Philippa's success was widely reported and helped to counter the prejudicial belief that intellectual activity was harmful to women's health, yet may not have helped the campaign, started in 1895 and led by Millicent, to admit women to Cambridge University degrees. A senate vote in favour of membership was crushingly defeated, and women were not granted Cambridge degrees until 1948.

There were, however, small steps towards educational equality. Rhoda's step-sister Amy Garrett, an active suffragette, was instrumental in making Bedales School, founded in 1893 by her new husband John Badley, the first genuinely co-educational English boarding school.

Millicent meanwhile continued to write and to speak on a variety of subjects, including working-class women's pay and conditions, the exploitation of children, female education, and of course women's suffrage. Following the defeat of the amendment to the reform bill of 1884, the outlook for women's suffrage was bleak. Nevertheless, she did much to bring together the various divided and decentralised organisations committed to the cause, and served on the committee that led in 1897 to the formation of the National Union of Women's Suffrage Societies (NUWSS). She became its president ten years later. From 1902 she was also active in the international suffrage movement, attending meetings all over Europe.

Although the suffragist campaign has since been eclipsed in the public imagination by the militant actions and suffering of the suffragettes, the commitment of the NUWSS to constitutional methods in fact won a larger and wider membership, especially among working-class women. Millicent never sought to undermine the Women's Social and Political Union, founded by Mrs Pankhurst in 1903, and acknowledged the effectiveness of their methods. Indeed, in 1906 Millicent, who condemned force-feeding as torture, hosted a banquet in honour of the first ten suffragette prisoners, and both Elizabeth and her daughter Dr Louisa Garrett Anderson actively supported the WSPU.

Millicent Fawcett leads a peaceful procession by the NUWSS from Embankment to the Royal Albert Hall on 13 June 1908.

In the years leading up to the First World War Millicent travelled the country constantly to speak on behalf of the cause. Although not a fan of marches, in the summer of 1913 she fully supported the Great Suffrage Pilgrimage organised by the NUWSS as a means to secure national publicity and support. Thousands of women walked along eight routes from all parts of the country, in some places meeting with violent protest – stones and rats were thrown at them and sleeping wagons threatened with torching. They converged on Hyde Park for a rally attended by fifty thousand people. Millicent then led a deputation to Prime Minister Asquith. Yet, despite winning sympathy for their orderly and peaceful tactics, she and her deputation went away empty-handed, and any hope of progress was further postponed by the outbreak of war the following year.

During the First World War, both the suffragists and the suffragettes agreed to transfer their energies to the war effort. Elizabeth's daughter Louisa, for example, helped establish, first, a series of military hospitals in France, all run by women, where she became a chief surgeon, and then the Endell Street Military Hospital in London. Although Millicent refused to support those in the suffrage movement who advocated pacifism, she continued her work to secure better pay and conditions for the increasing numbers of working-class women now employed in war-work.

When the question of franchise reform returned to the political agenda, it was impossible not to extend the vote to the returning soldiers. Millicent's question to the Prime Minister was clear: why deny it to the women who had supported the war with equal effort? A compromise was reached, with age and property qualifications to limit female enfranchisement so that, with so many men lost in the war, women would not outnumber men. Royal Assent

A triumphal drive after the passing of the 1928 Equal Suffrage Act,
Philippa Fawcett sitting behind her mother.

for the Representation of the People Act 1918 was granted
in February, and in March Millicent presided over a trium-
phant rally at the Queen's Hall, ending with the rousing
singing of 'Jerusalem'.

Neither Millicent nor her sisters had ever believed that
female self-determination could be achieved by the kind of
separatism advocated by other feminist pioneers in education or medicine. Far from establishing separate and parallel
spheres for women, the Garrett sisterhood had persisted in
joining men on equal terms and enabling other women to
do the same. At a time when middle-class 'women's work'
was seen as amateur and trifling, their great achievement
was to persuade by their own powerful and individual exam-
ples of professional ability and perseverance. In 1919, when
the Sex Disqualification Removal Act finally opened all
the professions to women, it was Millicent's younger – and
favourite – brother Samuel, a London solicitor who had
actively supported earlier challenges to the Law Society's

William Dring (attrib.), Dame Millicent Garrett Fawcett, 1927.
Millicent wears the robes of her Doctorate of Laws awarded by St Andrews
University in 1899, and a jewelled pendant presented to her in 1913
as President of the NUWSS.

refusal to admit women as solicitors, who ensured that his
firm was one of the first to employ female pupils.

She and her sisters had also amply demonstrated that
women could take on the responsibility of public office.
In 1901, for example, Millicent was appointed to lead a

government commission of women to investigate conditions in Boer War concentration camps, and in 1908 Elizabeth, having retired to Aldeburgh, became the first woman in England to be elected to the role of mayor.

In 1925 Millicent Garrett Fawcett was made a Dame of the British Empire. From a very young age, she had, with the active support of her father, husband and sisters, been able to overcome the supposed impropriety of a woman publicly making political demands, and went on to become, as one of her biographers wrote, 'the principal leader of one of the most important movements of modern times'. Her memorial in Parliament Square is well deserved.

In July 1928 Millicent was in Parliament to witness the passing of the Representation of the People (Equal Franchise) Act that finally gave women equal voting rights with men. She died in August the following year in the Gower Street home she had shared with Agnes for forty-five years.

Sources and acknowledgements

Elizabeth Crawford, *Enterprising Women: The Garretts and their Circle*, London: Francis Boutle, 2002

Jenifer Glynn, *Pioneering Garretts: Breaking the Barriers for Women*, London: Hambledon Continuum, 2008

Jo Manton, *Elizabeth Garrett Anderson*, London: Methuen, 1965

David Rubinstein, *A Different World for Women: The Life of Millicent Garrett Fawcett*, Columbus: Ohio State Press, 1991

Ray Strachey, *The Cause: A Short History of the Women's Movement in Great Britain*, London: Virago Reprint Library, 1978

With thanks to Miranda Garrett, Margaret Young and, as ever, Jean Gooder.

Susan Lawrence
(1871–1947)

JILL NICHOLLS

To be frank, I had never heard of Susan Lawrence. I asked around. A Labour Party activist friend recalled her name vaguely from a pub quiz: 'Wasn't she one of the first Labour women MPs?' A feminist historian friend: 'Wasn't she the one who wore a monocle?'

She was indeed one of the first three Labour women MPs, all elected in 1923 – and the first to speak in the House of Commons, opposing cuts in school meals. She was one of the first Labour women in local government too. As a councillor in the impoverished London borough of Poplar in 1921, she went to jail for 'contempt' in the famous Rates Revolt, when the Labour-led council refused to collect the full rate, arguing that the poor were being asked to pay for the poor.

She helped translate and wrote an enthusiastic preface to Trotsky's *Lessons of October 1917*, published in London in 1925. She addressed open-air meetings of a thousand workers in the East End during the General Strike of 1926. And she was the first woman to chair the Labour Party Conference, in 1930.

But she had not always been a socialist. She started out as a High Church Tory and did a volte face in 1912, when she was 40. She is sometimes dismissed as prudent, even a little dull, but it was a life full of surprises.

She was born Arabella Susan Lawrence in 1871, into a prosperous Conservative family, her father a solicitor, her mother the daughter of one judge and sister of two. After Francis Holland School in London, Susan went to University College London and then up to Newnham in 1895, where she roomed in Clough and read Maths. In 1898 she was among the 'senior optimes' in Part I but did not complete Part II, due to the sudden death of her father.

She was a striking figure. Her Newnham College obituary remembered her as

> tall, upright, dignified, a little older than the usual run of students, extremely short-sighted, aiding her vision by the frequent use of an old-fashioned lorgnette.* She had a piano in her room, though was not known to play it, and when bicycling started, kept a Dalmatian dog to accompany her as protection on her rides. Everyone was impressed by her great knowledge of books, history and public affairs, and no one was surprised when she became leader of the Tory Party in the College Political Society. Here she showed herself a keen debater, especially in her advocacy of Church and Empire.

For thirteen years after leaving Newnham, Susan remained a Tory. Through her involvement with church schools, she was elected a member of the London School Board in 1900, at the age of 29. In 1904, she joined the education committee of the London County Council and in 1910, was elected to the LCC as a Municipal Reform

---

*Later swapped for a monocle which apparently 'amused the factory girls, who adorned their eyes with pennies to imitate it, allowing them to fall to the ground with devastating clatter.' In fact, in the photographs I have seen, she is wearing quite disappointingly ordinary glasses, or none.

(Conservative) representative for the affluent, safe seat of Marylebone.

During this period, she would talk of 'wicked socialists'. Yet within two years, she had left the Conservative Party and turned to Labour. What caused this Damascene conversion?

We cannot know her thoughts or the reactions of her family and friends as her personal letters and papers were destroyed, with her home, in the Blitz. But there had been signs that her views were moving to the left. She'd been shocked by the low wages and poor conditions of school cleaners tolerated by the Tory-controlled LCC and by 1911 was said to be 'in full revolt against her party' for refusing to improve them. She had also met and made friends with the social reformers Beatrice and Sidney Webb, and in 1911 joined the Fabian Society.

But perhaps most significant of all was her encounter at this time with the charismatic Scottish trade unionist and feminist Mary Macarthur. Mary was to have a huge and lasting influence on her. Contemporaries called it 'devotion' and spoke of Susan's 'despairing misery' when Mary was diagnosed with cancer in 1920. Susan moved in with her until she died a year later.

Mary Macarthur, 1909.

Like Susan, Mary was from a Conservative

31

background. Born in Glasgow, she'd changed her political stance at the age of 21, when she discovered the dire conditions in which workers such as shop assistants lived. She climbed quickly to the top of the trade union movement, moved south, and in 1906 set up the National Federation of Women Workers to give a voice to the thousands of women barred by men from trade unions. In 1910, when she met Susan, she was organising in Bermondsey. She led Susan through the streets of East London to show her what real poverty was like. Her new friend joined the Federation. Susan's letter of resignation from the LCC spoke of the need for Poor Law reform and her change of position on religious schools, but she was really resigning so that she could work with Mary and the Federation to improve the conditions of London's 2,000 school cleaners. These women worked irregular hours, received no pay during school holidays, and were hired and fired not by the LCC but by school caretakers. The formation of a Federation branch for cleaners and kitchen staff led to a minimum wage of 14 shillings a week, holiday pay and direct employment by the LCC.

Within months of her resignation, Susan joined the Labour Party and was swiftly re-elected to the LCC as Labour representative for Poplar. She even moved to live just off the East India Dock Road.

But her transformation to union organiser was not immediately successful. Margaret Bondfield, a seasoned Federation organiser and later another in that first trio of women Labour MPs, remembered Susan's first speech to a factory-gate meeting as a near-disaster.

Susan's voice had not been trained for speaking to an East End audience, who treated her as a comic turn and roared with laughter. I felt ashamed of them, to treat a stranger so, but also felt there was something to be said for the girls, who had never before heard that kind of voice. I reported to Mary that Susan had pluck to stick it out, but that unless she altered the tone of her voice and got control of it, she would never hold a crowd. Susan did alter the tone, and did get voice control in a very short space of time, and could control crowds, inside and outside the Party, the LCC and the House of Commons. That horrible experience made her 'one of us'.

For the next decade, this 'educated, affluent rentier' (in the words of the *Oxford Dictionary of National Biography*) worked with Mary to organise working-class women in London. During the First World War, many were working in factories, replacing the men sent off to the Front. Susan became organising secretary of the Federation's War Workers Campaign, and also Fabian representative on the War Emergency Workers' National Committee. In 1918, after only six years as a member, she was elected to the new women's section of the Labour Party's National Executive.

But Susan wasn't radical enough for Sylvia Pankhurst. The only socialist, anti-war feminist in her suffragette family, and active, like Susan, in the East End during the War, Sylvia mocked Susan's 'magisterial air' and said scathingly: 'She was never a suffragist, but she was one of the first to receive the fruits of the struggle when women received the Parliamentary vote. Like many successful politicians, she preferred to mount the political ladder by a reputation for being moderate, leaving the noisy work to other people.'

Yet you could say that Susan now won her radical spurs. In 1919 she joined Poplar Borough Council, led by George Lansbury. Two years later, along with 29 other Labour councillors, she refused to collect the poor rate, arguing

Poplar women councillors, Susan Lawrence smiling at the back, leave triumphantly for prison, cheered by a supportive crowd, 1921.

that it was impoverishing the very people it was meant to help. The councillors were sent to prison.

Susan 'bore her five weeks in Holloway with an amused tolerance, jesting with the wardresses', according to her Newnham obituary. Her main complaint was that she wasn't allowed to smoke! She spent her time reading Tolstoy, writing a pamphlet on local taxation and singing the Red Flag along with supporters in the street outside. She left prison a Labour heroine. And in 1923, after two unsuccessful attempts, she won a seat in Parliament, for East Ham North. While Nancy Astor (Cons) and Margaret Wintringham (Lib) before her had effectively got their seats through their husbands, Susan got hers through sheer brains, drive and determination.

In the first-ever Labour Government in early 1924, Susan was appointed Parliamentary Private Secretary to the Board of Education, the prelude to ministerial office.

In Parliament, the manner of this 'cerebral, widely read product of Newnham' (*Oxford DNB* again) was initially off-putting to some. Ellen Wilkinson, herself elected for Labour shortly afterwards, wrote: 'Tall, cold, severe, plainly dressed, at first when she rose to speak, the House prepared for the worst, then they glimpsed the real Susan, the woman of delicate humour, of a merciless wit, of a logic they believed was only masculine, of a mind which drank in facts as some men drink whisky.'

For some years Beatrice Webb shared her London house with Susan (complaining of her 'barbaric, modern' taste in furnishings) and Susan was on the NEC with Beatrice's husband Sidney. But even she wrote that Susan:

> is a remarkable woman, more than 'well-to-do', with a forceful intelligence, presence and voice – more forceful than attractive … Is she lovable? I never heard of anyone being in love with her; I am inclined to think this lack of the quality of lovableness accounts for a certain recklessness, a certain dare-devil attitude towards life, as if she cared not whether she lived or died. She is an enraged secularist and would be a revolutionary Socialist if she had not a too carefully trained intellect to ignore facts, and far too courageous and honest a character to hide or disguise her knowledge.

The minority Labour government was short-lived. When Labour lost the election in late 1924, Susan lost her seat. But she was swiftly returned as member for East Ham in 1926.

During the General Strike that year, Beatrice Webb witnessed Susan at work in the East End. She was:

> in a state of emotional excitement – I might almost say exaltation. She had taken six meetings on Saturday and another half dozen on Sunday: 'A glorious spirit', she said, the world would never be the same again, never again would the workers be trodden underfoot as they are now. 'We are living in MOMENTOUS times, on the eve of great things … The men are splendid – we must and shall win.'

But the Strike was called off that afternoon. Beatrice Webb reflected on:

> the amazing change in Susan Lawrence's mentality from the hard-edged lawyer-like mind & conventional manner of the 'Moderate' member of the School Board whose acquaintance I had made 25 years ago to the somewhat wild woman of demagogic speech, addressing her constituents as 'comrades' and abasing herself and her class before the 'real' wealth producers.

To Beatrice, this was 'living in an unreal world. … To keep in touch with what she imagines to be the proletarian mind she has lost touch with facts as they are.' To Susan, it was following her principles and her heart.

In 1926 she gave £5000 of her own money to the miners' strike fund – a quite enormous sum at that time.

Now in Opposition, Susan strengthened her parliamentary reputation with virtuoso baiting of the Conservative Government. Her eye for detail and mastery of finance enabled her to make merciless attacks on Neville Chamberlain's de-rating Bill, using her height and manner to the full. She earned the nickname in *Punch* of Lady Susan Macbeth: 'Infirm of purpose, give me the daggers!' said one cartoon.

But Beatrice Webb had other things on her mind than Susan's virtuosity in debate:

> How eminently respectable are those three women Labour MPs (Susan, Margaret Bondfield and Ellen Wilkinson). You can barely think of any one of them having an 'intrigue' – even a flirtation. Margaret has her religion as relaxation; Susan and Ellen have their travels, their gossips and their smokes. They have many men friends; they may all have had offers of marriage; but I doubt whether any of the three has had a lover.

Caricature by Tom Cottrell of Lawrence in the House of Commons, 1929.

She shared an unkind joke about Susan being a 'virago intacta', saying it was 'as witty as it was true'. Of course many women in public life then remained unmarried, but how I would love to have found a lover, male or female, to prove Beatrice wrong!

When Susan retained East Ham at the general election of 1929, and the second (minority) Labour government was formed under Ramsay Macdonald, she got a ministerial post at last, as parliamentary secretary at the Ministry of Health. As a minister, she was said to be 'completely indifferent to pressure to present a "feminine" image … she took no interest in her choice of clothes, sending round to a department store for half a dozen inexpensive dresses to be sent to her office, and briefly raising her head from her papers, to select one by pointing with a pencil.' (*DNB*)

But she was a success, in her department and at the dispatch box, seeing the Widows' Orphans' and Old Age Pensions Bill through Parliament. She had to struggle with her conscience and make compromises, given the erratic economic policy of the embattled administration: she tussled with the thought of resigning. But in 1930, when she became the first woman to chair the Labour Party conference, she called for party unity.

Women Labour MPs elected in 1929, in the first General Election since the introduction of universal suffrage in 1928. Lawrence is third from the left, Margaret Bondfield next to her in the front.

However, when the Labour Chancellor proposed severe cuts in unemployment benefit, she publicly opposed them and resolved to resign if they went ahead. But the Government collapsed and Susan, like most Labour MPs, refused to take part in Ramsey Macdonald's National Government. She lost her seat in the 1931 General Election and was never again an MP. Her last attempt was in 1935, in Stockton-on-Tees, but she lost to the incumbent, one Harold Macmillan.

She had long been an intrepid traveller, when even for the wealthy it was far from easy. In 1924, she'd spent six months travelling around Soviet Russia, without becoming a convert. Now, in the 1930s, she went to the USA, where she was excited by Roosevelt's New Deal. In 1935, she travelled to Palestine, where she admired the 'Tolstoyan Jewish communes' and tried (without much success) to persuade the Labour Party Conference that a socialist utopia was being created.

The following year, a Royal Commission was set up to find out how the British mandate was working in view of growing strife between Jews and Arabs. Susan argued that the problems arose because Jewish development was so far ahead while the Arabs' needs were neglected. By 1938, she'd been persuaded by Labour leaders in Palestine to advise the NEC that some form of partition was inevitable.

It was one of her last contributions to the party she loved. In 1941 the Labour Minister Hugh Dalton was delighted when 'silly old Susan Lawrence' was ousted from the NEC – 'she should have retired gracefully years ago'.

Now she devoted much of her time to translating books into braille for the blind. She remained on the Executive of the Fabian Society till 1945. As the Labour politician Margaret Cole wrote: 'that genial old fighter' Susan became in her late years 'the happiest visitor at Fabian Summer Schools, when her racy anecdotes of the Great Ones of her own day were always immensely popular.'

Cole recalled that in mid 1945:

> I was lunching with her at Westminster; she was full of beans, and rubbing her hands she said 'My dear, isn't it delightful? The war's over. I have been good for years, but I've got a flat in London now and I'm going to have a party every week, and I'm going to grumble and grumble and grumble! Won't it be fun?'

She died in 1947, in her London flat. The once High Church Tory turned secular socialist was cremated at Golders Green a few days later.

'Gaunt of figure in her later years, with close cropped grey hair, piercing eyes and an engaging habit of darting a finger at one in conversation,' said *The Times*, 'she was the most transparently honest and unegotistical of politically minded women.'

More effective, more emotional and far more radical than I had expected, Susan Lawrence should be better known.

Portrait of Susan Lawrence by Walter Stoneman, 1930.

Note on Sources

I started of course with her Newnham obituary by 'M.E.G.' from the *Newnham Roll Letter* 1948.

I read Susan Lawrence's own words in her preface to Trotsky's *The Lessons of October 1917*, trans. S. Lawrence and I. Olshan, London: Labour Publishing Co., 1925; her *Letter to a Munition Worker*, Fabian pamphlet, 1942; and many Hansard entries.

I very much enjoyed *Beatrice Webb's Diaries* (both editions, ed. Norman & Jeanne MacKenzie and Margaret Cole) and Sylvia Pankhurst's *The Home Front*, 1932, repr. London: Cresset Library, 1987.

I also referred to David W. Howell's entry in the *Oxford Dictionary of National Biography*, 2015 and D.E. Martin's entry in the *Dictionary of Labour Biography*, vol.3, 1976.

I used 'Susan Lawrence: the Monocled Maverick' by Katherine Perera, in her *History of Labour Women*, which I found on www.labourlist.org, and also checked www.spartacus-educational. com and C.D. Rackham, *Fabian Quarterly* 57, Spring 1948, pp.20-3.

I scanned for references to Susan:
Martin Pugh, 'Class Traitors: Conservative Recruits to Labour 1900–30' in the *English Historical Review*, February 1998

Brian Harrison, *Prudent Revolutionaries*, Oxford: Clarendon Press, 1987

Elizabeth Vallance, *Women in the House*, London: Athlone Press, 1979

Jane Martin, 'Beyond Suffrage: Feminism, Education and the Politics of Class in the Inter-war Years', *British Journal of Sociology of Education*, 2008

Cathy Hunt, *The National Federation of Women Workers, 1906–1921* Basingstoke: Palgrave MacMillan 2014

Marjory Stephenson
(1885–1948)

ROSALIND RIDLEY

Marjory Stephenson was one of the most distinguished scientists to have studied at Newnham yet she is one of the least known. She was a pioneer in the emerging field of biochemistry, on the boundary between the biology of living things and the chemistry of molecular reactions, and an inspiring teacher to a whole generation of research students who carried on her work.

Her great contribution to science was recognised when in 1945 she became one of the first two women to be elected a Fellow of the Royal Society.

What was the research that so impressed those Fellows?

Marjory's work was concerned with the most fundamental processes of life. She studied bacteria because this meant she could work with whole organisms showing nearly all the basic chemical reactions essential for life, and they reproduced or died so fast that experiments could be carried out rapidly. The results she obtained in bacteria, particularly the existence and actions of enzymes – proteins that speed up chemical reactions – turned out to apply to almost all living organisms, including plants and animals.

Marjory's laboratory work was mainly concerned with biochemical processes that occur in the absence of oxygen, called anaerobic reactions. Anaerobic bacteria are found in the human body, for instance in digestive processes in the colon and in a sprinter's overworked calf muscle, as well as in sewerage plants and modern bio-digesters.

Her expertise in anaerobic bacteria could be of practical use. Could she explain a foul smell emanating from the River Ouse in Suffolk that was distressing local people? The engineer of the Ouse Drainage Board sent her a sample of mud from the river bed to examine and she and her team set to work. Marjory was able to show that the smell was due to an overgrowth of bacteria feeding on the effluent from sugar-beet mills, turning sulphates to sulphides – the same stink as rotten eggs – and producing methane, hydrogen and carbon monoxide from formic acid. Further studies established which bacteria were responsible for the reactions and the enzyme they were using to speed them up. So as well as helping to deal with a local problem, she was gaining fundamental insights into 'the machinery of life'.

Marjory also secured the future of her subject. As her citation for election to the Royal Society made clear, she stood out not only for her ground-breaking research but also for writing the first – and for many years the only – textbook on bacterial metabolism, and for training a number of graduate students who themselves went on to do first-class work.

Marjory was born in Burwell, Cambridgeshire, in 1885, the youngest of four children. Her father was a farmer with a practical and scientific understanding of agriculture and biology and a believer in Darwin. At her mother's instigation, Marjory and her sisters were educated at home by a 'beloved' governess, Anna Botright, and Marjory then boarded at Berkhamsted School for

Girls. Again encouraged by her mother, Marjory followed her somewhat older sister, Alice Mary, to Newnham and read chemistry, zoology and physiology from 1903 to 1906.

Most lectures in the University were not then open to women. So she was taught zoology in the Balfour Laboratory – a joint enterprise between Newnham and Girton Colleges – and chemistry, by the lively Ida Freund, in Newnham's own laboratory (now the 'Old Labs') in the college grounds.

But she was able to attend lectures on physiology in the University laboratories. One in particular made a deep and lasting impression. It was on the subject of lactic acid production and muscle contraction and was given by the biochemist Frederick Gowland Hopkins. Although much that he said was speculative, 'it opened a new world of thought' for her. Indeed it did, for she was to return some years later to work in his laboratory.

Marjory gained a Second Class in Part I of the Tripos and would have liked to pursue a career in medicine. But her parents were not able to provide the necessary financial support for such a long training so she had to find a means of earning her own living. This she did by training in, and then teaching, domestic science at Gloucester Training College and as a visiting lecturer at Cheltenham Ladies' College, and then at King's College for Women in London.

Domestic science may seem a light-weight alternative to a career in medicine but, at that time, education about nutrition, hygiene and sanitation was extremely important. Since there were no antibiotics, no electric household refrigerators and very little domestic central heating, careful household management was often a matter of life and death, especially for children. Nonetheless, Marjory did not like teaching it and in 1911 she obtained a position at University College, London, to work with Dr Robert Plimmer in his new biochemistry laboratory. She was funded by a personal Beit Fellowship to study digestive enzymes in animals and published two papers in the *Biochemical Journal* in 1912 and 1913; a third, written with two other Beit fellows, on diabetes in a canine model, was published in 1915.

By that time, the public-spirited Marjory was working for the war effort in France – and was back to domestic science. She had volunteered in August 1914 for service with the Red Cross and was serving as a cook with the Voluntary Aid Detachment (VAD), initially in Rest Stations in France. There was nothing routine about this job. On 2 November 1914, despite having only three Primus stoves on which to boil water, her kitchen managed to provide meals for 2,300 exhausted and wounded soldiers who arrived unexpectedly from Ypres. In 1915, she was promoted to Head Cook

Miss Stephenson during her time as Chief Commandant of VADs in Salonika, 1916–18.

and worked in two hospitals in Normandy before travelling to Salonika in Greek Macedonia to organise kitchens and set up a nurses' convalescent home. She became Chief

Commandant of the VADs in Salonika and stayed until June 1918, serving for two years in challenging conditions without a break.

'Very capable and hard-working and very competent as Principal Commandant' wrote Colonel H.L. Fitzpatrick, area Commissioner for the Red Cross, who judged her character 'excellent'. She was awarded the MBE and the Associate Royal Red Cross medal. Her experiences during the First World War made her an ardent pacifist.

After the war, in January 1919, she joined the research group of the man who had so inspired her as an undergraduate. Now Professor Gowland Hopkins (but known as 'Hoppy'), he was head of the Biochemical Laboratory in Cambridge, where she worked for the rest of her life. Hopkins encouraged her to move from animal nutrition to the study of bacteria.

She became an Associate and later a Fellow of Newnham, taking an active part in the governance of the College.

At first Marjory was financed by the remaining part of her Beit Fellowship but she was then funded mainly by the Medical Research Council (MRC). This was renewed annually until 1929 when Sir Walter Morley Fletcher, the first Secretary of the MRC, made her a member of the Council's External Scientific Staff (ESS) with a tenured position. This and an inheritance from her father, who had died that year, made her financially independent.

In 1930, she published the first edition of her book *Bacterial Metabolism*, which remained the standard textbook in the subject for many years. Her pioneering research and her uniquely thorough textbook made her one of the founders of the subject of biochemistry, for which Cambridge University awarded her the title of Doctor of Science (ScD) in 1936.

Staff of the Cambridge Department of Biochemistry, Marjory second from right in the front row, Prof. Gowland Hopkins in the centre, 1930.

The MRC was, and remains, a largely gender-blind employer. The ESS category of employment allowed individual researchers to pursue their own scientific projects within a university department without being overburdened by administration or teaching, or being directed scientifically by anyone else. Marjory, who by now was universally known as 'MS', described this situation as 'peculiarly attractive to me'.

This privileged position may at least partly explain why she did not transfer to the academic staff of the Biochemistry Department until 1943, when she became a University Lecturer, even though she had been lecturing to Part II students since 1925. Another reason may have been that she was not particularly good at formal teaching. As her student and later collaborator, Ernest Gale recalled: 'Revere her as we may, no-one could call her a brilliant lecturer. The lectures might well begin in the middle and end at the beginning. But at least we gathered that someone had done something terrific. At least you went away and read all about it.'

She was, however, very good indeed at teaching and inspiring her research students one to one, in the lab, although she expected them to work independently. She considered it vital to 'train new workers': scientists engaged in research should teach not only for the good of students but for the good of their own work and the future of their science. Many of her students went on to achieve distinction. Ernest Gale, for instance, became professor of chemical microbiology at Cambridge. She was also particularly welcoming to political refugees such as Hans Krebs in the lab; he judged her 'scientifically the best of the whole lot' and went on to become professor of bio-chemistry at Sheffield and then Oxford.

She could be explosive when others fell short of her own high standards. 'MS was forthright and believed in striking while the temper was hot', said Gale. 'There were days when we tiptoed round the lab, hoping that lightning really did not strike twice.' But apparently the storm soon passed and the normal cheerful atmosphere returned. Such a robust but quixotic nature is often regarded as essential in a creative laboratory.

In 1945, Marjory Stephenson and Kathleen Lonsdale, a crystallographer, were the first two women to be elected as Fellows of the Royal Society. As might be expected, the election of women to this ancient society had proved a difficult issue (see p.52ff.); it was finally settled by a referendum of the Fellows. But once the change had been approved there was little doubt that Marjory and Kathleen were candidates of the highest calibre. There were other female candidates that year but they were not elected.

In the same year, Marjory was a founding member of The Society of General Microbiology (now The Microbiology Society) and was elected unanimously as its second President in 1947, following Sir Alexander Fleming. The Marjory Stephenson Memorial Lecture is given biennially at the Society in her memory.

By the end of the Second World War she had become an international figure in her subject. In 1946, she was invited to speak in Paris at the Congress celebrating the 50th anniversary of the death of Louis Pasteur, one of the scientists she most admired. At home, she had become Secretary of the MRC Committee on Chemical Microbiology, set up in 1943 to co-ordinate work and make proposals for new studies. She also devised a new Part II course in microbiology as part of the Cambridge biochemistry course. By 1947, there was so much work being done on bacterial metabolism that a new building known as the 'The Bug Hut' was opened next to the main building of the Biochemistry Department in central Cambridge. Marjory ran that building and was appointed Reader in Biochemistry, the highest position then available for someone who was not Head of Department.

In parallel with her scientific career, Marjory had an active and enjoyable private life. Perhaps as a result of her extensive catering experience, she developed what her Newnham obituary described as 'a masculine appreciation of good food and wine' and was a first-rate cook. She enjoyed many outdoor activities including horse riding, travelling and gardening. In 1935, she purchased a plot of land in Latham Road, near the botanical gardens in Cambridge, and organised the construction of a house around which she planted an orchard, becoming expert in the cultivation and propagation of fruit trees. Indoors, she was an avid reader, painted in oils and enjoyed the company

Marjory and her dog Judith outside the laboratory, 1920s.

of friends, who always spoke of her with affection and respect.

Marjory was diagnosed with breast cancer when she was 59 years old and died four years later, in 1948. At the time of her death, the third edition of her book *Bacterial Metabolism*, which she had completely rewritten because so much progress had been made in the field, was being prepared for publication. In the introduction, she described her research as being underpinned by a desire to 'catch sight of the machinery of life'.

In her obituary in the journal *Nature*, the biochemist Dorothy Needham said: 'One of her great qualities was her hatred of any form of cant, hypocrisy, pretension or slovenliness; she was ruthlessly outspoken in her condemnation of any such suspected defect'.

But her many friends remembered her warmth and generosity too. Margaret Whetham Anderson, her first PhD student and lifelong friend, described Marjory's personality in her Newnham obituary as:

> envigorating, perhaps to be likened to a fire in the hearth, shedding a generous inspiring warmth and glow, sparkling with wit and vivacity, yet with scorching disdain for any shiftiness, jealousy or insincerity … her uncompromising speech scarcely concealed a true tenderness of heart.

Marjory Stephenson working in the lab, probably in the 1930s.

What took the Fellows so long? A note on the Royal Society and women

It can sometimes take a long time for clever people to get their heads round the obvious. In the case of the Royal Society, four decades elapsed between the first, unsuccessful, attempt to elect a woman (Hertha Ayrton in 1902) and the successful election of Marjory Stephenson and Katherine Lonsdale in 1945. Admittedly there were two World Wars and the Great Depression during this period, as well as huge changes in women's suffrage, employment rights and place in society. But confusion and casuistry surrounded the issue.

At the creation of the Royal Society in the seventeenth century, women had not been mentioned and were thus not specifically barred. Paradoxically, this may actually have hindered progress. The records suggest that the Fellows felt they needed to give themselves permission to elect women before they could bring themselves to do it.

From the end of the nineteenth century until the end of the First World War, there were various unproductive discussions about creating a supplementary charter to establish the eligibility of women since there was no bar that could be symbolically removed. Then, in 1919, the Sex Discrimination (Removal) Act cleared the way: it required that women be eligible for many positions, including election to learned societies.

So why wait another two decades? Mainly because it was felt necessary to make such a substantial move only with the support of the whole membership.

There were three strands of support for the election of women: gender equality, common justice and the pursuit of academic excellence.

The geneticist J.B.S. Haldane, a great egalitarian and feminist, was motivated by gender equality. In 1943, he wrote in *The Daily Worker*, the Communist newspaper of which he was an editor: 'The most striking omission in this list is the name of any women. There are probably not 50 British women worthy of the FRS. There are certainly half a dozen. The Society has no colour bar; it cannot exclude women indefinitely.'

The biochemist Charles Harington, an old-fashioned and highly principled man, was motivated by his great sense of justice, of which gender equality was just a logical component. Henry Dale, the President, believed that scientific excellence was paramount and that this could best be pursued by including highly competent women.

Thomas Merton, the Treasurer, suggested that a poll of the Fellowship be taken because of the implied 'break in the traditions of the Society' but Henry Dale feared this innovation would be 'imperiling the whole structure of government of the Royal Society'. In the end there was a postal poll and 89.4% of the votes cast were in favour of the election of women.

Then the Society had to be confident that women of high enough calibre would be nominated to ensure that the election of the first women would be successful. They decided to have more than one female candidate because the non-election of a single female candidate (on grounds of lack of merit) might make it look as if the membership did not wish to admit women.

In the event, they put forward several candidates of outstanding

Portrait of Marjory Stephenson FRS by Mrs Campbell Dodgson, commissioned by Newnham College to mark her election to the Royal Society in 1945.

merit and the biologist Marjory Stephenson and the physical scientist Kathleen Lonsdale were both elected.

The record of the event says: 'The admission of women into the Fellowship of the Royal Society … far from being a breach of tradition, may be acclaimed as a natural measure to be adopted by a society constituted for the promotion of natural knowledge.' And in his Presidential address in 1946, Henry Dale said the election of women merely involved a 'perfectly normal adjustment … to the growth in extent and distinction of women's contribution to the advancement of science by research'.

In other words, there had not, after all, been a radical change in tradition in the Society; there had merely been a change in the level of involvement of women in science. Well, fancy that.

Note on Sources

Obituary by Margaret (Whetham) Anderson, student and life-long friend of MS, in *Newnham College Roll Letter* of 1949

Biography of MS by Dr Jane Cope, Newnham alumna and biochemist (and former head of the National Cancer Research Institute), on website of Cambridge University Department of Biochemistry; also 'Marjory's War', a separate essay by Dr Cope about Marjory's experiences in the First World War

S. Štrbánová, *Holding Hands with Bacteria: the Life and Work of Marjory Stephenson*, New York: Springer, 2016

E. Shils and C. Blacker, *Cambridge Women: Twelve Portraits*, Cambridge: CUP, 1992

J. Mason, 'Commentary on The Admission of the First Women to the Royal Society of London, 1946', *Notes and Records of the Royal Society of London*, vol.46, 1992, pp.279-300

Francesca M. Wilson
(1888–1981)

SUSIE HARRIES

Francesca Wilson – humanitarian, history teacher, traveller – was someone it would be easy to caricature. She was the kind of woman who routinely attracts the label 'indomitable', whether she was adopting Russian orphans, crossing Macedonia on a mule, or encouraging shell-shocked Serbs to make baskets from raffia. Her living quarters were littered with cat hair, festering milk bottles and the stubs of cork-tipped cigarettes cut in half, and for most of her life she surrounded herself, in the words of one friend, with 'deserving foreigners of an interesting kind'.

In her biography of Eglantyne Jebb, founder of Save the Children, Wilson mourned a dying breed of Victorian maiden aunts, and she might well have been taken for one, but she was in fact a modern figure – a beginning, not an end. She was one of the first of a new class of international aid worker, active in the aftermath of every major European conflict for five decades. Contemptuous of the 'Lady Bountiful' approach to relief work, she devoted herself – as a career, not a hobby – to improving the prospects of the displaced and the dispossessed, certainly with immediate practical help but also, and perhaps more importantly, with publicity.

From Belgium in the First World War to occupied Germany after the Second, by way of the Spanish Civil War and the Hungarian Resistance, she opened canteens, staffed kitchens, set up workshops and children's colonies – and then she wrote and spoke about it, as a tireless public campaigner for the cause of refugees. She was relentless in pursuing other people's good. 'She used everybody she knew for everybody she knew', in the words of Fred Wolsey, her protégé, amanuensis and, ultimately, carer.

Francesca was (in her own view – photographs do not bear this out) the plain and clumsy one of four children born into a Quaker family in late Victorian Newcastle. Her father was a hatter's furrier and it was a conventional middle-class upbringing, blighted only when her mother was persuaded by a fervent nursery maid to become a member of the Plymouth Brethren. Clever, conceited and thoroughly unpopular at school (again, by her own account), Francesca escaped to Newnham in 1906, to find it initially a disappointment.

She had elected to change from Classics to History, in the belief that this would broaden her outlook on the modern world, only to find the course dusty and pedestrian, with little opportunity for impassioned intellectual discussion – her favourite occupation. Nor, in Old Hall – which she described as 'at that time the dullest of the Newnham houses ... [with the] reputation of being good at games and Christian Union activities' – was she making the intimate friendships of which she had dreamed. It would have annoyed her to realise that hers was a common predicament – failing to be adopted by the high-flyers she wanted to know whilst fending off the lesser souls who would readily have accepted

Francesca Wilson at Newnham, 1909.

her. She left Cambridge with second-class honours and a teachers' certificate in 1912, to pursue an uninviting career as a history mistress.

It was while she was teaching at a school in Gravesend in 1914 that she met her first refugees – a pitiful huddle of Belgian women and children on a quay in Tilbury – and presented herself to a Quaker relief agency as a volunteer to go to France. Shrewdly, they suspected her motives, which she would herself diagnose as 'the love of excitement and adventure, the itch to meddle in other people's affairs, the nostalgia for foreign countries and for increased scope for one's powers'.

The agency declined her services, but they also under-estimated her persistence, and before long Francesca had made her way to a Dutch punishment camp for Belgian officers and their families. Thwarted in her ambition to teach the men English as a means of whiling away their captivity – they were, she complained, too busy planning escape tunnels – she supervised the women in the making of mattresses from ticking and a seaweed stuffing.

Unrewarding as this was, it confirmed her in the belief that the most effective form of relief was to enable self-help. The temporary doles – food, clothes and medicine – were important, but for Wilson the key to lasting recovery and resettlement was useful work. Having nothing to do was her own worst nightmare, and she would devote the next thirty years, in the intervals of teaching and writing, to providing refugees of all ages with the means of planning for the future and regaining their self-respect. In Serbia in 1919 it was war casualties returning to their homeland – *grands mutilés*, whom she soon had making artificial limbs. In Spain in 1937 it was those dispossessed by the Civil War – elderly men set to sewing rope-soled sandals, and adolescent boys kept out of trouble through vegetable gardening in a farm colony by the sea.

It was while she was working with Polish refugees in Hungary in the autumn of 1939 – founding a Girl Students' Home and galvanising the inmates of intern-ment camps to run classes in carpentry and art – that she became involved with the Budapest underground which was helping stateless Czechs to flee the Germans. Arrested and questioned by the Hungarian secret police in May 1940, she made a hasty escape when it seemed that the invasion of Britain was imminent. '"I ought to be in on that," I thought,' she wrote later. 'But would I get there in time?'

She spent the war working for refugee organisations in London. But in the autumn of 1945 she was in Germany under the auspices of the newly-founded United Nations Relief and Rehabilitation Administration (UNRRA), as one of their first officers to arrive in the American zone to work with a new category of displaced persons – the victims of the concentration camps.

For all her thirty years' exposure to human misery, degradation and loss, she had never encountered anything to equal the sights and sounds of the Föhrenwald camp outside Munich, peopled mostly by survivors of Dachau. Nor had she come across relief work as run by the American military – lacking, she felt, in 'the improvisation and empirical dash' which had made those hectic years in the Balkans after the First World War so enjoyable. It would be her last effort as a field worker.

From now on Wilson would further the refugee cause as a writer and propagandist. Her aim was to change the ways in which people displaced by war and famine were viewed by the settled and secure, and to alter the methods by which relief agencies sought to help them. Her principal tactic was to personalise problems by telling the stories of individual refugees – in articles for the *Manchester Guardian*, at the moment when serious newspapers had their greatest audiences; in radio talks, on the Home Service and Third Programme; in public meetings up and down the country. In books such as *In the Margins of Chaos* (about relief work all over Europe, from Serbia to Spain, 1914–40) and *Aftermath* (France, Germany, Austria and Yugoslavia, 1945–6) she used her own story to argue for a new direction in international aid.

A small pamphlet – *Advice to Relief Workers: Based on Personal Experience in the Field*, published immediately after the war – sets out her views succinctly. This was a new age of planning, and, for better or worse, relief had moved on from the benevolent free-for-all which had sometimes turned voluntary aid in the First World War into 'an undignified scramble for the disabled and shell-shocked', with well-intentioned but unqualified workers competing in compassion. Aid efforts must be co-ordinated, and they must lay foundations for the

A rare image of Francesca Wilson in her middle years, 1940s.

future. Avoid supplanting local services, she argued, train local officials, help the inmates of displaced persons camps to help themselves. Learn languages, master basic survey methods, gain a little knowledge of the most modern nutritional technologies – and show some humility.

This was a message addressed to her peers: 'Women are more quickly intoxicated by power than men,' she wrote firmly. 'The unaccustomed authority which the control of goods in short supply gives them, often turns their heads. I have seen women who have begun well, turn overnight into dictators.'

Her message for the longer term, however, was aimed at a wider audience – at the inhabitants of a country that

could well afford to offer permanent shelter to refugees.
There should be some kind of Geneva Convention for
refugees, she maintained, and a relaxation of the laws
restricting the admission of aliens to Britain. Her pamphlet *Displaced Persons – Whose Responsibility?* (1947) was
directed at teachers, debating societies and discussion
groups, and sought to change attitudes. Who should be
responsible for looking after displaced people? Should
they be forcibly repatriated – to the new Soviet Union,
for example? Was Britain doing enough? Should it open
its doors wider – and if it did, what effect would this
have on British workers? These were issues that the
people of Britain should think about; and they should
consider the benefits, and not simply the costs, of
accepting refugees.

In World Refugee Year (1959–60) she published *They
Came as Strangers*, an account of immigrants to Britain,
from the Flemish weavers of the fourteenth century to
the Jewish academics exiled by Hitler, and all that they
had brought with them in terms of art, science and
industry. In an appendix to the book she set out a way
in which the displaced persons camps of Europe might
be made redundant: individual British citizens should
each 'adopt' a refugee, and towns or communities might
'adopt' a whole camp and become responsible for its
clearance.

Romantic as this proposal might have sounded,
Wilson was not counselling anything she had not herself
tried, with her own series of transients. In her first years
as an aid worker, she had taken two Belgian girls into her
home to improve their prospects, and in the 1920s she
took in a succession of Russian boys with a view to giving
them security and an education. Once again, she had

no illusions about her motives. She never pretended she would not have liked to be married and have children, and her 'adoptions' were a means of providing herself with 'an ersatz family': 'They gave me what I needed … people to care for, an interest outside myself, a redemption from myself.'

They Came As Strangers was dedicated to 'all the Exiles who have enlivened my Home'. The Russian boys of the 1920s were followed in the 1930s by Jewish refugees from Nazi Germany. Wilson was then living in a largish house in Edgbaston, teaching history at a Birmingham girls' school, and she opened her doors to a sequence of lodgers who included the ill-matched pair of German art historian Nikolaus Pevsner and the White-Russian-turned-Marxist philosopher Nikolai Bakhtin. What Pevsner and Bakhtin did have in common was that, at the moment when Wilson took them in, they were at a very low ebb: as a landlady, she would always have most sympathy with the down and out. Her last thirty years were spent in London, in another tall, scruffy house, this time in Fellows Road, Hampstead, which was invariably filled with young boarders – aspiring actors, musicians, artists, all desperate to work in the London of the 1960s, none able to pay a commercial rent. They earned their keep with cleaning and house repairs, and there was an honesty box by the telephone.

In a *Guardian* article on the perils of adoption, Wilson had insisted there was no place in that particular relationship for gratitude; the child should owe its adoptive parent nothing, and in self-defence the parent should try to remain emotionally detached. This was not a philosophy with which she personally had much success. 'I am, I think, on the whole more loving than loved', she wrote.

Francesca Wilson in the 1970s.

'Not always, but on the whole. Probably one is richer that way, however painful at times.' She was talking here primarily of romantic love – of the lovers she had had over the years (most of them, including Bakhtin, foreign: 'It was rather a matter of luck if Francesca liked you if you were English,' one friend remembered.) In other kinds of attachment, she was much better off.

She died in Hampstead of a stroke at the age of 93, to be remembered with a mixture of amusement, admiration and deep affection by nieces, their families, and a wide range of friends and ex-lodgers.

Her public reputation as a campaigner for refugees, and as an aid expert through personal experience, was largely behind her by the 1970s, but she remained a force to be reckoned with. Asked once for a radio talk to pick a character from history whom she would have liked to be, she had gone for a Renaissance woman at the court of the Duke of Urbino – attractive but accomplished, and educated well enough to hold her own in conversation: 'To have all those wonderful minds discoursing round your fire ….' When working on famine relief in Vienna in 1923, she had met Sigmund Freud ('a very accessible person … willing to talk about his theories'); and through Bakhtin she had welcomed Wittgenstein to her country cottage in 1938 (he was taken aback by its austerity).

Intellectual discussion remained her passion to the end of her life, and as an old lady with erratic sleeping habits she was not above banging on the floor at three in the morning to summon one of her lodgers for political or philosophical debate.

She adored party games, at which she cheated, and she did not hesitate to pick flowers and fruit from other people's gardens if they looked like going to waste. She demanded lifts without shame – 'Nice for people to have the chance to do a good deed' – and at ninety, she said her only regret was not to have been put in prison for her beliefs. 'She was a real trial, and I liked her very much,' wrote one friend. Both sentiments would have pleased Francesca.

Note on Sources

The most extensive piece of writing on Francesca Wilson is the PhD thesis (University of Birmingham, 2010) 'Place, Life Histories and the Politics of Relief: Episodes in the Life of Francesca Wilson, Humanitarian Educator Activist' by Sián Roberts, who also wrote Wilson's entry in the *Oxford Dictionary of National Biography*.

For personal information, I have drawn on *Francesca Wilson: A Life of Service and Adventure*, a partial memoir by Wilson herself, edited by her niece June Horder (privately published, 1993), with reminiscences from friends and relations.

An interesting blog by Ellen Ross for the *Journal of Victorian Culture Online* sets Wilson in the context of women's philanthropy. http://jvc/2014/06/02/thinking-about-francesca-wilson-and-the-victorian-imaginery-that-surronded-her/

Alix Strachey
(1892–1973)

JANET BURROWAY

There are rare persons who are creative, productive …
but insist on staying anonymous. Alix Strachey was
such a being … a colleague who both served and enriched
psychoanalysis, but did so silently, almost anonymously.' So
said M. Masud R. Khan in his eulogy of Strachey at the
British Psychoanalytical Society a month after her death.
'All talk with tenderness and relish about her, yet nowhere
does one find enough of a narrative about her to define
her person for oneself.'

This elusive and contradictory quality is a leitmotif of
the scant and scattered comments recorded about Alix
Sargant-Florence Strachey. To Quentin Bell she was
'austere and melancholy'; to Lou Andreas-Salomé 'my
poor beautiful Red Indian'; to Frances Partridge 'the best
conversationalist, the most fluent and logical thinker', with
'a fierce look'; to James Strachey 'an absolute boy' – whom
he would eventually marry and dote on. Sigmund Freud
referred to Alix and James as 'my translators', yet on the
title pages of the massive 23-volume *Standard Edition* of
'the Professor's' works, translation is credited to James
alone, merely 'assisted by' his wife. To a degree this wifely
modesty suggests the mores of the times. Yet everyone who

knew them understood that Alix was at least as responsible as he for the bringing of psychoanalysis to the English-speaking world, in both its substance and its meticulous expression.

Alix Sargant-Florence Strachey was born in Nutley, New Jersey on 4 June 1892, the second child of the British painter Mary, née Sargant, and the American musician Henry Smyth Florence. The parents had met and married in Paris, where both were studying their respective arts. Both came from liberal and progressive backgrounds, though Mary from a significantly wealthier and more distinguished family than he. Four years after meeting and a year after marrying they emigrated to Nutley, where Henry helped found an artist's colony, and the two children Philip and Alix were born.

But when Alix was only six weeks old her father drowned in a swimming accident. Her mother Mary had never liked America (she sailed to England several times during the few years she lived there), and when Henry died she returned immediately and permanently to her homeland. Alix grew up travelling back and forth between her mother's studio in Chelsea, the Continent, the seaside, and the family home in Sussex. When she was six, her mother bought Lord's Wood in Buckinghamshire (a plot of land she wanted to rename Lady's Wood – but that was a step too far for the times), and built a house in which they settled.

Mary was an ardent feminist, but Alix refused the trappings of girlhood with a ferocity her mother found hard to handle. She adamantly refused to wear the ruffled fashions then considered appropriate, used her dolls for spear-throwing practice, and once poured ink on a tutor's trousers – very possibly because Philip was being taught Greek and Latin and she was not. In spite of her long eventual marriage to and intense work with James Strachey, throughout her life Alix's chosen colleagues, and probably a few of her lovers, would be women.

Alix was enrolled as a part-time boarder in a London prep school in 1902, and two years later entered Bedales School, where for an unknown reason she lasted only a few weeks, though she re-enrolled the following year and successfully settled. This staccato pattern was one that would dog her throughout her life because of her own or others' illness or incapacity.

Her mother had pressed both Alix and Philip to become artists, and in 1910 the daughter was enrolled in the Slade School of Art – but painting was clearly not her métier. Apparently she was early interested in progressive politics, for that year James Strachey met her for the first time at the Summer School of the socialist Fabian Society, and wrote to his brother Lytton, 'The women were a shocking lot, – except for a delightful Bedalian (Miss Sargant-Florence!) an absolute boy.'

Alix entered Newnham in 1911 and 'wasted herself' (Philip's opinion) on modern languages. She learned French, Italian and enough German to acquaint herself with Freud's works, though they were not of course on any reading list. At nearly six feet, Alix had been strong and even beefy as a teenager, the only girl on the Bedales School cricket team. At Cambridge she came under the influence of an American classmate named Jessie Holliday, turned vegetarian and lost weight at an alarming rate – a result of what would probably now be diagnosed as anorexia nervosa. She spent the summer in a sanatorium and was forever after spectre-thin.

At Cambridge her mood was dark. She was known as witty and gregarious on the outside, troubled within, and

Newnham Cricket XI, Alix Sargant-Florence far right, 1912.

she later wrote mordant poetry about her desolation there. Virginia Woolf described the 'pitchy black of her horizon' and mocked that, 'she wants to work at something that matters to no one; & will never be used, seen or read, & can be done for no more nor less than three hours a day.' If Virginia was right, Alix signally failed on all counts.

There were exciting discoveries too. Philip, also at Cambridge, had become acquainted through the Heretics Society, the Apostles and *The Cambridge Magazine* with many of the crowd that would become the Bloomsbury Group, and he introduced Alix to these intellectual and political lights, including again the brothers Lytton and James Strachey.

Alix and Philip both took undistinguished degrees, she a year behind him, in 1914, and that summer Alix treated herself to travel in Europe, Finland and Russia – her passage home blocked in this last by the beginning of the First World War. What could she do when hostilities trapped her in Russia? Why, learn Russian, of course. And how to drive a car.

Back in London again, she shared a house with Philip in Mecklenburgh Square, Bloomsbury, and honed her intellectual and social skills on that progressive, pacifist, atheist and sexually permissive company: among them Rupert Brooke, Virginia Stephen and Leonard Woolf, Dora Carrington, Ralph Partridge, Vanessa Bell, John Maynard Keynes, Augustus John, Bertrand Russell, and of course the Strachey brothers.

Alix and James now reconnected at the 1917 Club, so named to mark the Russian Revolution. 'Met Alix again,' James wrote to Lytton, and, several meetings later, 'Alix is lovely too', later still, '… a rather good brain; but dull my God and ponderous to a degree.'

Alix had an affair with David 'Bunny' Garnett, who registered 'her intelligence, her coldness and her apparent detachment', and she was for a time involved, purely sexually, with Harry Norton, 'every ten days in order to free his suppressed instincts!' she said. James had been in love with Rupert Brooke, and was now pursuing pretty Dora Carrington. But at this point Alix fell hard and set out to win him. Her method was to engage James intellectually (perhaps not so ponderously), a passion Carrington could not match. Virginia saw Alix's pursuit as calculating but so relentlessly driven that 'she deserves to win'.

In 1919 Alix rented 41 Gordon Square and invited James to live there as her roommate, free of charge: '… alas poor Alix', wrote Mark Gertler, who had also experienced adoration of Carrington, 'What a sickly thing love is!' It was probably Alix who had introduced James to, and now intensified his interest in, the writings of Freud. She said, somewhat disparagingly, of *The Interpretation of Dreams* 'this so-called Dream-Work is a great deal indebted to waking intelligence.' Yet she translated Freud's long essay on 'The Uncanny' ('Das Unheimliche') for *Imago* magazine in crystalline English prose. James for his part was interested, like many intellectuals of the period, in psychic matters, and increasingly in their connection to Freud's teachings. He and Harry Norton joined the Society for Psychical Research and James sought the advice of Ernest Jones on becoming a psychoanalyst. Jones told him to begin with medical school, so James enrolled, lasted three weeks, and dropped out to find some other way.

In 1920 James and Alix decided to take a European tour, and since they could not afford separate hotel rooms as society required and their passports indicated, they got married. James wrote to Freud in Vienna and pleaded for an extended analysis, offering a very minimal £1 an hour. On the grounds that James wished to be a psychoanalyst, Freud accepted this reduced fee. So after several weeks of touring, James and Alix settled in Vienna to stay for James's analysis, which, he wrote

Alix and James Strachey en route to Vienna, 1920.

to Lytton, was 'sometimes extremely exciting and sometimes extremely unpleasant … sometimes you lie for the whole hour with a ton of weight on your stomach simply unable to get out a single word.'

One evening at the opera Alix suffered a panic attack, which resulted in her asking Freud if he would accept her as a patient too. Freud, though initially reluctant to treat both members of a couple, agreed, and later grew enthusiastic about the potential additions it might make to psychiatric knowledge.

However, a case of flu complicated by pleurisy and bronchial pneumonia sent Alix to a sanatorium, where a section of her ribs was removed – without anaesthetic – to clean her lungs. Carrington went to Vienna to look after James who 'is very exhausted', she said; but Alix refused to see her. Freud meanwhile, although Alix had not finished her analysis, declared that both she and James were ready to be psychoanalysts and, after recuperation in warm climates, they went back to England to hang out their shingles. They arrived 'much in love', as Michael Holroyd reports in his massive *Lytton Strachey*, 'playing chess and translating Freud'.

On this they were now spending serious time, committed to 600 pages of 'case studies,' and when that project was completed and delivered to the young Hogarth Press (which would eventually publish the entire Freud canon), Alix went to Berlin at Freud's suggestion to take up further analysis with Karl Abraham. That she delayed the analysis shows her devotion to the translation; that she left James for the better part of two years, her belief in analysis.

It was a great time to work with Abraham. Analysis was at its peak of popularity in a city where sexual decadence, art, and excess were the norm, a Berlin later described by George Grosz as 'gaily-coloured froth that many people took for the true, happy Germany before the eruption of the new barbarism'.

The letters Alix and James exchanged during her stay in Berlin in 1924–5 present the most intimate existing portrait of their marriage, although they contain few sexual references and no information whatever about what went on in the analysis – a respectful adherence to the rules.

Though Alix had pursued James fiercely, she is the more romantically reticent of the two. 'I'm more in love with you than either of us bargained for,' James declares, and, 'Dearest love, all of this, and everything else, is only a stop-gap to help bridge the gulf between now and Easter.' After he visited her, she wrote, 'I wish you were here & I could give you a kiss – when you are here I never seem to make the most of it …' But she discouraged him from a further visit in May, in order to concentrate on her psychoanalysis.

Though we know little of her analysis in Berlin, Alix's letters make clear that she read constantly, in English, French and German (at one point she was reading both Thomas Mann and *Sherlock Holmes* in German), attended weekly or bi-weekly concerts and lectures, visited galleries and art openings. But she also loved dancing, and sent James notes of her conquests on the dance floor that may have been intended to inspire jealousy or may simply represent the free and easy nature of their relationship.

The child-analyst Melanie Klein was also a patient of Abraham's; Alix sought her company, and they became frequent companions and good friends. In Berlin, Klein was attacked by a coterie of male analysts who denigrated the notion of child analysis (and probably the whole idea of a woman psychoanalyst). Alix defended her fiercely and (in spite of considerable reluctance from Ernest Jones) arranged a series of lectures at the Psychoanalytical Society in London. Alix speculated that she might have 'Sapphic emanations of a dim, dim kind' towards Klein but also found her a disorganised and sloppy lecturer, and fretted over translating her manuscripts for the British salon: 'She's a dotty woman', Alix wrote to James. 'But there's no doubt whatever that her mind is stored with things of thrilling interest.' The lectures were so success-ful (largely due to the Stracheys' efforts) that Klein soon moved to England. Yet Alix continued to find Klein too cheerful for her own dark views of the human condition. 'Oh dear, her heart is too nice for the likes of me.'

In her letters Alix can be capable of class and national snobbery: the Germans are 'very, very simple-minded,' and the Swiss 'utterly devastating in their dullness'. She speaks of 'one of those awful officer's wives', the 'stupid brutalized faces' of the bicy-cle riders in the *Sport-Palast*, and most scornfully of 'a very resolute female' who held forth on 'the general impossibility for women to have any judgment' on the topic of politics. Sometimes it seems her mockery is laced with her own lack of confidence: she speaks of a party of 'pseudo-intellectual

Alix in the garden, late 1920s.

Bohemians ... very pretentious, tiresome and vulgar ... Or perhaps they weren't so bad. Only I̲ felt contemptuous & also very stupid.' Often she longs for home and the brilliant Bloomsbury life: 'I do think the English splendid in their madness ... & nobody outside has any Ahnung [inkling] of it. I miss it terribly.'

1925 saw three significant milestones in the Stracheys'
lives: the publication by Hogarth Press, on the same day
as Virginia Woolf's *Mrs Dalloway*, of their translation of
Case Studies; James's entry into analysis in London with
James Glover; and the protracted illness and death of
Karl Abraham in Berlin. Alix waited in Berlin through
his illness, then had no option but a return to London,
her second analysis also unresolved.

Now began, however, a long and apparently more
settled life, as well as a moderately affluent one, with
both wife and husband practising as analysts, both being
analysed themselves (after the death of James Glover, by
his younger brother Edward), and undertaking together
the great work of translating Freud's entire oeuvre.

Alix ultimately had greater regard for Freud's theories
than for the actual analysis she had experienced with him,
and she was not blind to the fissures in his thinking or her
profession. Remarkably, she said of Virginia Woolf that
her imagination was so interwoven 'with her fantasies –
and indeed her madness – that … it may be preferable to
be mad and be creative than to be treated by analysis and
become ordinary.'

The Stracheys' social life continued with the same
erratic and thrilling Bloomsbury folk as they had known
from Cambridge and, in some cases, even from Bedales.
They lived at Gordon Square until the beginning of
the Second World War, then repaired to Lord's Wood,
where they lived out their lives, an eccentric but revered
couple. Frances Partridge in her delicious diaries marks
the trajectory from one to the other, seeing them arrive
at the Partridge house, Ham Spray, 'two dark-clad figures
drooping across the lawn, like suits of clothes on hangers'
and 'they arrive in their little beetle car, with pale and

exhausted faces looming through the darkness.'

'Alix can't cook and refuses to try,' observes Partridge, 'so they take their ration in corned beef and eat it at table so close to the sink that they can reach out and hold each dirty plate under the tap'. But by 1952 her admiration is extreme:

> Alix and James have been and gone, leaving me full of admiration for Alix. She is the most intelligent woman I know, the best conversationalist, the most fluent and logical thinker – I don't feel she has received enough recognition for this fact … Throughout the weekend hearing her talk was pure joy.

The Stracheys would live at Lord's Wood, in the house Alix's mother had built and in which Alix grew up, until they died, James in 1967 and Alix in 1973.

Perhaps because of the enormous commitment to the translation project, Alix wrote only two original books, but in both she succinctly connected her Freudian understanding to political aims. In *The Unconscious Motives of War* in particular, she goes clearly through the stages of child development to show how infantile desire proceeds through the unconscious and conscious toward action, and how identification with a group,

Alix Strachey in her seventies, a passport photo.

like sleep or hypnosis, leads to a regression back through these processes toward infantile thought. The Church, the Army, secret societies, even schools (which 'oblige the middle-classes to conform to their standards'), can produce an immature warlike us-against-them stance. Having lived through the Second World War and seen the dangers of nationalism, she reasons that the sovereign State is the most aggressive of such groups; its leaders, whether dictatorial or elected, are inevitably influenced toward the authoritarian.

Often she could be speaking to today's audience: 'An immediate change from an authoritarian to a liberal regime can, of course, be forcibly imposed … against the will of its people', she writes, but such a change will be detested because it is enforced by a foreign state. She is referring to the Weimar Republic, but might be talking about Iraq or Afghanistan.

Again, the book ends with an admonition that could be aimed at our current world and its threat of nuclear holocaust:

> … a true and full knowledge of just how complete that extermination will be should be brought home to everybody by every possible means, and as soon as possible. This is the first task of statesmen and scientists.

Alas, when Alix proposes a solution to the problem of war, she can only argue for universal analysis, because when people understand their mental processes better, they own and control them better. But, however unrealistic, her proposal does show how strongly she believed in the power of analysis to give people clarity and hope amid the encircling gloom. She could take pride in her role in introducing it to England, though it seems she was too modest to do so.

Note on Sources

Biographical works on Alix Strachey are thin on the ground, though she figures in many accounts of Bloomsbury, and her credited translations and original work are, though largely out of print, available online as articles and in used book sites. She figures fully but invisibly throughout *The Standard Edition of the Complete Psychological Works of Sigmund Freud* and is credited as sole translator of some few Freud articles and others by Melanie Klein and Karl Abraham. The fullest account of her life I found is in the Meisel and Kendrick collection of *The Letters of James and Alix Strachey 1924–25*. Among the sources I found most useful are these:

M. Masud R. Khan, obituary address at a Scientific Meeting of the British Psychoanalytical Society, 16 May 1973

Michael Holroyd, *Lytton Strachey: The New Biography*, New York & London: W.W. Norton & Co., 1995

Perry Meisel and Walter Kendrick, *Bloomsbury Freud: The Letters of James and Alix Strachey 1924–1925*, New York & London: W.W. Norton & Co., 1990

Frances Partridge, *Diaries, 1939–1972*, London: Phoenix Press, 2001

Alix Strachey, translator, 'The Uncanny', by Sigmund Freud, in *Imago*, 1919.

Alix Strachey, *The Unconscious Motives of War: A Psycho-Analytical Contribution*, London: George Allen & Unwin Ltd, 1957

Jacquetta Hawkes
(1910–1996)

UNA McCORMACK

'Brilliant and beautiful and perceptive.' That was how Sir David Attenborough remembered, in 2009, the female star of the first television programme he worked on as a young trainee producer at the BBC in the 1950s.* It was the series *Animal, Vegetable, Mineral?* – a popular panel show in which archaeologists, art historians and other experts were asked to identify interesting objects from museums. And the woman he was describing was Jacquetta Hawkes.

During her lifetime, Jacquetta Hawkes was a highly recognisable public intellectual. As well as regular television and radio appearances from the 1950s onwards, she was well known for her bestselling book *A Land* (1951), a unique personal history of the island of Britain from the pre-Cambrian rocks to the Bomb. More notoriously, perhaps, her very public divorce in 1953 from her first husband, the eminent archaeologist Sir Christopher Hawkes, in order to marry J.B. Priestley, was a press sensation. She remained extremely active – as a broad-caster, writer, lecturer, journalist, and activist – for the

* Sir David Attenborough, 'Personal Histories' (transcript), 12 October 2009, Babbage Lecture Theatre, University of Cambridge

rest of her life. But she was unknown to me, her patrician style no doubt deeply unfashionable with commissioning editors during the 1980s. You cannot quite picture Jacquetta Hawkes on Channel 4.

As I researched my subject – visiting her huge archive, held alongside her second husband's in Bradford, reading the biography written by Christine Finn, the person who has done the most to keep Jacquetta's work alive – I became increasingly astonished at the breadth of her activities, as journalist, novelist, poet, lecturer, broadcaster, and polemicist, as communicator of ideas for popular interest, campaigner for nuclear disarmament, governor at the British Film Institute, and so on and on. This productivity and activity continued more or less up to her death. It is sad to reflect – as we often do with women's lives – how quickly she disappeared from popular memory. Her lifetime covered the expansion and proliferation of television and popular science books; her gift lay in bringing to life the past for a lay audience. Her writing – if idiosyncratic and now somewhat dated – nevertheless rewards reading.

A childhood picture of Jacquetta shows her, typically tomboyish, clambering up the gate-post of the family home in Grange Road. Jacquetta had a quintessential Cambridge childhood. Born Jessie Jacquetta Hopkins on 5 August 1910, her father was the eminent biochemist Sir Frederick Gowland Hopkins, whose work was foundational to the emerging discipline of biochemistry, and who was awarded the Nobel Prize in 1929 for the discovery of vitamins. (Jacquetta, in her *Desert Island Discs* interview from 1980, calls them in her dry, marked RP, 'vytamins'.) Her mother, Jessie Anne Stephens, was a gifted and dedicated nurse who pioneered infant welfare in Cambridge after the First World War. Jacquetta was the youngest of their three children, with a much older brother and sister. Shortly after her birth (in 'a corner of Emmanuel College'), the family moved to 71 Grange Road, a house built for them, an easy walk to her father's lab and college (he became a fellow of Trinity in 1910, the college adapting their statutes to accommodate his agnosticism).

The setting of the house on Grange Road, which at that time was on the very edge of the city, encouraged Jacquetta's affinity with nature: her childhood notebooks record her rambles around the area, with painstaking ink drawings of flora and fauna encountered. Even more, the site of the house stimulated her interest in the past, lying, as it did, at a point where an Anglo-Saxon cemetery had been built over a Roman road.

Tomboy Jacquetta in the garden of 71 Grange Road, Cambridge.

The sight of an amber necklace, found in the grounds of the house, and held at the Museum of Archaeology and Anthropology, inspired Jacquetta's interest in archaeology at an early age (including an illicit late night dig by torchlight, excavating the lawn).

Educated first at a dame school, and then at the Perse High School for Girls, Jacquetta's schooldays were not her most successful period. An air of mild exasperation rises from successive school reports, as teachers complain about her carelessness, lack of application, how much better Jacquetta could do if only she would *work*. She bucked somewhat against authority, founding a Trespassers Club, with points awarded for the (non-damaging) invasion of others' property, and preferring not to wear uniform or to participate in organised games.

The end of Jacquetta's schooldays coincided, fortuitously for her, with the launch of a new archaeological Tripos at Cambridge, the only full degree course in the country. So she applied to Newnham (where her sister Barbara had studied), and was interviewed by the principal, Miss Strachey. Jacquetta recalled having a bad cold, which she made a great deal of during her interview. After a short conversation, Miss Strachey dismissed her, saying, 'Well, Miss Hopkins, I think you had better be *tottering* home.' But Jacquetta had done enough: she went to Newnham (without a scholarship), becoming the first woman to study for the relatively new degree of Archaeology and Anthropology.

Jacquetta's friend from her college days, Peggy Lamert, recalled that she 'stood out like a star'. She was beautiful, coolly intellectual, and extremely attractive to both men and women. There were several proposals of marriage, none of interest. Jacquetta later recalled, 'My first two proposals came from men who had motor cars and shared my interest in ornithology … My "bird-watching" became something of a joke among my Newnham friends.' At the end of Jacquetta's second year, however, she joined a dig at Camulodunum, near the Roman city of Colchester. The director of the excavation was a brilliant young man with a reputation for acquiring glamorous girlfriends, Christopher Hawkes. Hawkes, at the time an assistant keeper at the

British Museum, would, in 1946, become Professor of European Archaeology at Oxford. Jacquetta was naturally flattered by the attentions of this confident older man; Hawkes, in his turn, made heavy weather in letters to his rather snobbish mother of Jacquetta's charm and famous father. He continued to court Jacquetta throughout her final year at Newnham.

That was the year in which hard work finally paid off, and Jacquetta gained first class honours. On the basis of this, she won the Gladstone Travelling Scholarship, and went out to Palestine to excavate caves on Mount Carmel. This excavation, directed by Dorothy Garrod, discovered the first Neanderthal skeleton outside Europe. The whole experience had a profound and lasting effect on Jacquetta, and inspired some of her most visionary prose, in her book

Dorothy Garrod and Jacquetta in Palestine, 1931.

Man on Earth (1954), expressing the depth of her experience of connectivity through time:

> I was conscious of this vanished woman and myself as part of an unbroken stream of consciousness, as two atoms in the inexorable process to which we all belonged … With an imaginative effort it is possible to see the eternal present in which all days, all the seasons of the plan stand in an enduring unity … But there is also a terrible reality in that opposing vision of the linear passage of time, of the continuous leaving behind which fills us with a cruel awareness of the wastage of our brief lives. Perhaps, of all men, the archaeologist must be most aware of time passing … So, while we uncovered the skeleton detail by detail, and then shrouded it in plaster of Paris, I often looked at it in sorrow.

On her return, in 1932, Jacquetta and Christopher became engaged. There were many warning signs that this was not going to be a successful marriage. Hawkes' mother did not see Jacquetta as wholly suitable. There was intense pressure on Jacquetta for a formal church wedding, to which she eventually – and tearfully – capitulated. Jacquetta's mother repeatedly asked if she was sure. Nevertheless, they married at Trinity in October 1933. In her late novel, *A Quest*

Marriage of Jacquetta to Christopher Hawkes, 1933.

of Love (1980), Jacquetta recalls the honeymoon in frank, almost cruel terms:

> We quite enjoyed our honeymoon in Majorca: it was neither a joy nor a disaster … While I came nowhere near to passion, it would not be just to say that I proved frigid or altogether indifferent. I wanted to please my husband and even gained some little pleasure in the attempt. Of course this was not enough … As it was we enjoyed the sun, the bathing and visiting antiquities – and were not unhappy. Similar words might be used to describe the following years of our marriage.

On their return to London, the newlyweds settled to a pleasant if not luxurious existence in London, working together at a dig at Gergovia, near Clermont-Ferrand in France (1934), visiting Lascaux, attending conferences in Scandinavia (1936), and working together on *Prehistoric Britain* (1937). From the outside they appeared a model, modern professional academic couple, although stresses of work caused exhaustion in Christopher, and there was a headlong clash with his mother at one point. Their son, Nicholas, was born in 1937. A joint excavation – with Nicholas and nursery maid – happened in Hampshire, in 1938, and, in the summer of 1939, Jacquetta led her first solo excavation in Waterford in Ireland. She continued work on her own book, on the archaeology of Jersey, published in 1939. Jacquetta's career as an archaeologist was, thus far, following the standard course for her generation (the requirement for a doctorate being at the time non-existent), with solid work and publications.

And then came the war. Christopher was seconded to the Ministry of Aircraft Production. Jacquetta became a civil servant at the Post-War Reconstruction Council. After

Jacquetta on excavation in Ireland, 1939.

a brief stay in Dorset (where Jacquetta fell in love with her host, Betty Pinney), Jacquetta took Nicholas to her parents in Cambridge, remaining in London during the week. With Christopher working late at nights, Jacquetta made her own social life. Her old college friend, Peggy Lamert, introduced her to the poet and critic W.J. Turner.

Jacquetta's affair with Walter Turner was the first passion of her life. He was almost sixty when Jacquetta met him; she was thirty. The affair (Turner was also married) brought about a profound sexual and creative awakening for Jacquetta. She began seriously to compose poetry: her archive holds a dense file, typed on thin wartime paper, of carefully crafted poems, some of which would later be published in a slim, luminous volume, *Symbols and Speculations* (1949). In 1946 Turner died suddenly of a brain haemorrhage, a devastating blow to Jacquetta. Christopher, in a beautiful letter which does him great credit, wrote to console her over her loss. She published no more poetry.

Life could not – and did not – return to the way it had been. After the war, Jacquetta moved to the Education Ministry, where she became an 'established principal', and was put in charge of visual education, including film-making. In 1947, she joined the British delegation at the six-week inaugural meeting of UNESCO in Mexico. Prior to the trip, she protested, to no avail, at the inclusion of a middlebrow author about whom Turner had been scathing – J.B. Priestley. As secretary to the delegation, Jacquetta found herself in regular communication with Priestley; they met first at a UNESCO meeting in Paris in July 1947 (Priestley, after this meeting, memorably described Jacquetta: 'Ice without and fire within'). At the end of 1947, the delegation left for Mexico. The affair began in earnest.

The period that followed was one of the most productive and creative of Jacquetta's life. She was archaeological adviser to the Festival of Britain in 1951, contributing as 'Theme Convenor' for the display on 'The People of Britain'. In 1950, she became a Governor of the newly-established British Film Institute (she went on to provide the commentary for the arresting 1953 experimental film on Barbara Hepworth, *Figures in a Landscape*, directed by Dudley Shaw Ashton, with Jacquetta's words spoken by poet Cecil Day-Lewis and a score by Priaulx Rainier). She co-wrote a (not entirely successful) play, *Dragon's Mouth*, with Priestley in 1952. And she wrote and published the book for which she remains most remembered: *A Land* (1951).

Robert MacFarlane, in his introduction to the 2012 reprint of *A Land* (pp.xi–xii) calls the book:

> a missing link in the British tradition of writing about nature and the landscape … a geological prose poem; a Cretaceous cosmi-comedy; a patriotic hymn of love to Terra Britannica; a neo-Romantic vision of the country-side as a vast and inadvertent work of land-art … I can imagine it re-performed as a rock opera.

It is a remarkable book, unlike any other I have read, taking the reader from a moment in which Jacquetta lies on the ground one evening in Primrose Hill, sensing the earth beneath her, back to the formation of the rocks that will eventually become the island of Britain, and on through prehistory, history, custom, tradition, all told in Jacquetta's intense style. The overall effect is kaleidoscopic, deeply visual and poetic. Much of the scientific content has dated, but the overall vision – of the deep connection of the present to the past – sings from the page. Part history, part hallucination, it was hugely successful.

Jack and Jacquetta married in 1953. Their divorces were very public. But the marriage – her second, his third – was

Marriage of Jacquetta Hawkes and J.B. Priestley, at Caxton Hall Westminster in 1953.

intensely happy. They made their home first in the Isle of Wight and, from the 1960s onwards at Kissing Tree House, outside Stratford-upon-Avon, where they wrote prolifically and entertained extensively. Jack, much influenced by Jung, attributed the success of their marriage to the balance of the masculine and feminine elements between them; Jack's extroversion and Jacquetta's introversion; his intuition and her intellectualism.

Rachel Cooke, in her essay on Jacquetta in her book *Her Brilliant Career*, suggests that the marriage had a constraining effect on Jacquetta's talents, and that she never fulfilled the promise of the genius exhibited in *A Land*. Perhaps not, but there is no doubt that her intellectual and creative life continued uninhibited. Even a small time spent with Jacquetta's archive shows the dazzling range of her activities. She did not stop writing – both her own projects and with Jack (their 1955 book *Journey Down a Rainbow* recounts their separate trips around the United States: Jack to the consumer paradise of Texas; Jacquetta to the pueblos of New Mexico). She was 'archaeological correspondent' for various newspapers, and continued to publish popular works of archaeology up to the 1980s.

Her reputation within the academic archaeological community, however, was not sustained: her visionary style was entirely out of step with the scientism of the 1960s. Her novel *A Quest for Love* (1980) not only dealt frankly with her marriage and divorce from Hawkes, but used reincarnation as a device to link an Everywoman from pre-history through a lesbian Victorian affair to the autobiography at the end. It's a startling, albeit not entirely successful book, and did not help her academic standing.

She writes other novels. She delivers lectures on landscape to the Brontë Society. She edits a series of educational children's books with titles such as *Why the Past is Always Present*. A letter in her archives gives a tantalising glimpse of a TV series that might have been, in the late 1960s, had the producer concerned not had her energies diverted towards a 'project with Kenneth Clark'. And, in the midst of all this she finds time to be active – with Priestley, their friends Diana and John Collins (canon of St Paul's), and others she helps found the Campaign for Nuclear Disarmament in 1957, and she writes numerous pamphlets in support of CND. (She also somehow finds time to be governor of not one, but two schools.)

After Priestley's death in 1984, Jacquetta moved to Chipping Camden. She seems to have become more austere and daunting in her old age, perhaps frustrated by increasing infirmity. Her mind remains active. Her last book, *The Shell Guide to Archaeology* (1986) is written when she is well into her seventies, and contains asides at one of her bugbears, radio carbon dating. She was broadcasting into the early 1990s. She died on 18 March, 1996, and her ashes are buried close to Jack's in the Yorkshire Dales.

How then, should we assess Jacquetta Hawkes' contribution? As an archaeologist, she was increasingly out of step with the post-war mainstream emphasis on establishing a scientific grounding for her discipline. Her visionary, almost mystical, views were seen as a throwback to an earlier age. The novels have largely dated, although they are enjoyable. She was critical of 'Women's Libbers', making her not easily adopted by a contemporary cause. But her speeches, lectures, and various non-fiction works are crisp and engaging, and the poetry is beautiful.

Recently, she has begun to find a new readership, aided by the scholarly work done on her archive and through publications and presentations by Christine Finn.

A reprint of *A Land*, in 2012, with an introduction by Robert MacFarlane, positions the book within a tradition of visionary British landscape writing dating back at least to John Clare. Rachel Cooke's essay picks her out as an outstanding woman of the 1950s.

It is perhaps as a public intellectual that she is of most interest. In this, she was amongst the first of her kind – a woman speaking with authority, on a wide-range of subjects, in a lucid and intelligent voice, through a variety of mass media, thus reaching a huge audience. Women slip rapidly out of cultural memory. Our habits of thought keep men's work alive, while women become buried. Jacquetta is certainly worth reading, and undoubtedly worth knowing.

Sources and Acknowledgements

My grateful thanks to Jacquetta's authorised biographer, Dr Christine Finn, for her help with this piece as it was in progress. My thanks also to Dr Catherine Hills, for a fruitful and interesting discussion about Jacquetta's legacy as a populariser of archaeology, and the reasons for her eclipse. Thanks also to Alison Cullingford, who hosted my visit to the Hawkes Archive at Bradford University, and provided stimulating discussion while I was there.

Diana Collins, *Time and the Priestleys: The Story of a Friendship*, Stroud: Alan Sutton, 1994

Rachel Cooke, *Her Brilliant Career: Ten Extraordinary Women of the 1950s*, London: Virago, 2013.

Christine Finn, *Celebrating Jacquetta Hawkes*, http://jacquetta-hawkes.wordpress.com

Christine Finn, *A Life Online: Jacquetta Hawkes, archaeopoet*, http://humanitieslab.stanford.edu/ChristineFinn/Home; archived

Christine Finn, 'Jacquetta Hawkes and the Personal Past', BBC Radio 3 Sunday Feature, 3 August 2013

'Hawkes, (Jessie) Jacquetta (1910–1996)' by Christine Finn, *Oxford Dictionary of National Biography* (2004-09-23)

Jacquetta Hawkes, *A Land*, repr., London: Collins, 2012

Jacquetta Hawkes, *A Quest of Love*, London: Chatto & Windus, 1980

Jacquetta Hawkes, *Man on Earth*, London: The Cresset Press, 1954